The Best 50
BANANA RECIPES

David Woods

D1557437

BRISTOL PUBLISHING ENTERPRISES
Hayward, California

©2005 Bristol Publishing Enterprises,
2714 McCone Ave., Hayward, California 94545.
World rights reserved. No part of this publication
may be reproduced in any form, nor may it be stored in a retrieval
system, transmitted, or otherwise copied for public or private use
without prior written permission from the publisher.

Printed in the United States of America.

ISBN: 1-55867-312-1

Cover design:	Frank J. Paredes
Cover photography:	John A. Benson
Food stylist:	Randy Mon

BANANAS—THE BACK STORY

Banana plants are grown in practically all the tropical areas of the world. Native to Southern Asia, bananas were one of the first cultivated fruits. Today, they are the third most popular fruit in American markets, ranking just behind apples and oranges. Yet except for a small Hawaiian crop, the entire U.S. supply of this tropical fruit is imported, primarily from Central America.

Bananas don't grow on a tree but on a plant, which is really an herb. Why are bananas so readily available? Like pears, they actually ripen better off the plant. Consequently, they can be picked and graded in the tropics, shipped while still green and easy to handle, then ripened domestically in specially equipped rooms.

There are two principal commercial varieties of bananas, though you probably won't find them labeled as such. Mild-flavored Gros Michel, a long banana with a tapered tip, is very resistant to bruising but sensitive to tropical disease. Disease-resistant Cavendish, also mild flavored, is a curved banana that's more sensitive to bruising.

A look through the banana section of many U.S. markets reveals quite a few newcomers.

Easy-to-spot Red Spanish or Red Cuban bananas have purplish-red skin and sweet, creamy flesh. Saba and Brazilian are very straight, clear yellow bananas with squared-off sides and a prominent blossom end. They're tart even when ripe, astringent when unripe.

Short, stubby, pale gold Manzano, Apple, or Finger bananas come in bristly bunches. They're refreshingly tart, crunchy when ripe, but puckery if green.

Plantains resemble bananas, but they're longer, thicker, and starchier in flavor. In their native countries, plantains are used more like a vegetable than a fruit; they're usually baked or fried and served like potatoes. They are not suitable for eating raw unless very ripe, when they turn completely black.

NUTRITION: Bananas are an almost perfect food. A fully ripe large banana contain only about 100 calories; it's very low in sodium, high in potassium, high in fiber and a good source of Vitamins A, B_6, folic acid, in addition to an impressive list of other nutrients. And they're included on low-fat and low-cholesterol diets. Because of their low protein content, bananas are often recommended for hypoallergenic diets. The banana is often one of the first solid foods offered to infants and one of the last solid foods managed by the aged. High digestibility, lack of chemical irritants and delicate flavor make it important in special diet for the sick as well as for the healthy.

SEASON: Bananas are available year around.

SELECTION: For eating, raw, common yellow bananas may be firm and greenish yellow to clear yellow with a few black spots, depending on personal preference. Soft, black-spotted bananas are best for mashing to use in baked goods; firm ripe fruit is for most other recipes.

RIPENING and STORAGE: Ripen bananas at room temperature, uncovered, out of direct sun; turn daily. Bananas can be kept in the refrigerator to arrest the ripening process, but may lose flavor and texture. Chilling will turn the peel brown, but the fruit inside remains delicious. If you find yourself with a surplus of bananas, let them ripen naturally, then mash, add a little lemon juice to prevent darkening and freeze in an airtight container.

PREPARATION: Simply pull back the peel to eat out of hand, or remove peel and fibrous strings and then slice. Coat cut bananas with lemon, lime or orange juice to prevent darkening. To mash soft ripe bananas for cooking, peel and slice then mash with a fork or potato masher.

AMOUNT: Two large or 3 medium-sized bananas equal about a pound.

Ninety-eight percent of all American households buy bananas regularly. That's more than twenty pounds a year each. And that's good, because bananas are good for just about everybody. And they're okay on a reducing diet, with 85 calories in a $3\frac{1}{2}$-ounce banana. All that, and they're in a natural, portable package. You can't ask for much more from a food. Bananas make eating easy and delicious. This book contains a few ways to use them to make the day more nourishing.

My recipes are designed for common bananas; exotic types are best eaten raw. Use firm-ripe bananas when slices are called for; when you need mashed bananas for recipes use soft-ripe fruit.

FIRM BANANA OMELET

Makes 4 servings

Serve with your favorite pancakes or hash-brown potatoes.

1 large ripe banana
6 eggs, lightly beaten
2 tbs. half-and-half
2 tsp. brown sugar or honey
2 tbs. butter, margarine, or vegetable oil

In a medium bowl, mash banana until pulpy. Combine with eggs, half-and-half and brown sugar. Mix well. Place a large 12-inch, heavy skillet over high heat until very hot then turn heat to low. Melt butter in skillet, making sure sides are coated. Pour in egg mixture, cover, and cook for about 5 minutes. If top of omelet looks runny, lift edges with spatula, tilt pan, and let uncooked egg flow beneath cooked portion. Cover again and cook until eggs are set. Slide onto warm plate, fold, and serve immediately.

SUNRISE FRENCH TOAST

Makes 4 servings

This breakfast treat can be served with fresh fruit, jam, or your favorite syrup.

¼ cup orange juice
½ cup mashed ripe banana
3 eggs
¼ tsp. allspice

2 tbs. margarine, divided
8 slices whole wheat bread
confectioner's sugar, for dusting
warm pancake syrup

In a shallow bowl, combine orange juice, banana, eggs and allspice; mix well. In a large nonstick skillet, melt 1 tbs. of the margarine over medium heat. Dip both sides of 4 slices of the bread into egg mixture. Cook bread about 2 minutes on each side until golden brown. Repeat with remaining margarine, egg mixture and bread. Sprinkle with confectioner's sugar and serve with warm syrup.

BANANA FRENCH TOAST

Makes 4 servings

Serve these for breakfast or as a dessert with your favorite ice cream.

4 eggs
½ cup mashed ripe banana
¼ cup skim milk
1 tsp. allspice

1 tsp. vanilla extract
2 tbs. margarine
8 slices whole wheat bread
honey or warm maple syrup

In a shallow bowl, combine eggs, banana, milk, allspice, and vanilla; mix well. In large nonstick skillet, melt 1 tbs. of the margarine over medium heat. Dip both sides of 4 slices of bread into egg mixture. Cook bread about 2 minutes on each side until golden brown. Repeat with remaining margarine, egg mixture and bread. Serve with honey or syrup, if desired.

BANANA QUICHE

Makes 6–8 servings

A slice with hot tea or your favorite drink makes a perfect light lunch.

3 tbs. grated Parmesan cheese
1½ cups shredded Swiss cheese
1 baked 9-inch piecrust
1 cup diced bananas
3 eggs

1½ cups whipping cream
¼ tsp. grated fresh ginger
⅛ tsp. ground nutmeg
⅛ tsp. ground black pepper

Heat oven to 350°. Sprinkle cheeses evenly in bottom of piecrust. Top with bananas. In a medium bowl, beat eggs, cream, ginger, nutmeg and pepper until thoroughly mixed. Pour over bananas. Bake for 45 minutes or until set. Let stand 10 minutes before cutting.

BANANA AND ZUCCHINI QUICHE

Makes 6–8 servings

The banana and zucchini make this hearty dish just right for a summer breakfast or brunch.

8 eggs
1/4 cup milk
1/4 tsp. ground ginger
1/8 tsp. ground cardamom
1/4 cup grated Parmesan cheese
1/2 cup shredded Swiss cheese
1 baked 10-inch piecrust

1/4 cup chopped green onions
1 medium zucchini, coarsely grated
1 cup diced bananas
1/4 cup grated Monterey Jack cheese

Heat oven to 350°. In a large bowl, beat eggs, milk, ginger, cardamom and Parmesan. Set aside. Sprinkle Swiss cheese evenly in piecrust, then green onions, zucchini and bananas. Sprinkle with Jack cheese. Pour egg mixture over all. Bake for 25 to 30 minutes, or until center is set. Cool at least 10 minutes before cutting. Serve warm or chilled.

BANANA PANCAKES

Makes 6 servings

For banana lovers, this recipes provides a double shot of their beloved fruit.

1 ripe small banana, mashed
3 cups buttermilk
3 large egg whites
2½ cups flour
2 tbs. sugar
⅛ tsp. ground cardamom
1½ tsp. baking powder
1 tsp. baking soda
6 tbs. (¾ stick) butter, divided
4 ripe medium bananas, thinly sliced
warm maple syrup

Whisk mashed banana, buttermilk and egg whites in a large bowl to blend. Whisk flour, sugar, cardamom, baking powder and baking soda in a medium bowl to blend. Gradually whisk flour mixture into buttermilk mixture until well mixed.

Heat oven to 200°. Melt 2 tbs. of the butter in large nonstick skillet over medium heat. Pour batter by 1/2-cupfuls into skillet, spaced well apart. Place 8 banana slices on each pancake, spacing evenly. Turn pancakes when holes appear on the top, and bottoms are browned. Cook on second side until pancakes feel firm when pressed.

Transfer pancakes onto a cookie sheet; keep warm in oven. Repeat with remaining butter, batter and banana slices. Serve pancakes with warm syrup.

BANANA CRAISIN COCONUT PANCAKES

These tropical pancakes are snap to make.

1 cup all-purpose flour
1/2 cup whole wheat flour
2 tbs. brown sugar
1/2 tsp. ground cardamom
2 tsp. baking powder
1/4 tsp. baking soda
2/3 cup skim milk

1 tbs. vegetable oil
2 eggs
2 ripe medium bananas, mashed
1/2 cup flaked coconut
4 tbs. (1/2 stick) butter, divided
1/4 cup craisins (dried cranberries)

Combine flours, sugar, cardamom, baking power and baking soda in a large bowl. Beat together milk, oil, eggs, bananas and coconut in a medium bowl. Add milk mixture to flour mixture and mix well. Add 2 tbs. of the butter to a large skillet over medium heat. Pour 1/4 cup batter for each pancake into skillet; sprinkle with craisins. Turn pancakes when holes appear on the top, and bottoms are browned. Cook on second side until pancakes feel firm when pressed.

BANANA PAPAYA BISCUITS

Makes 36 biscuits

These fruity biscuits are sweet and taste lovely with peanut butter.

3 ripe small bananas, mashed
1 cup milk
2 tbs. oil
4 1/2 cups flour
1 tbs. baking powder
1/2 cup minced dried papaya

Heat oven to 450°. Lightly oil a cookie sheet. In a large bowl, mix bananas, milk and oil together. Add flour and baking powder and mix well. Stir in papaya. Place dough on a floured surface and knead for 3 minutes. Using a rolling pin, roll dough to a 1/2-inch thickness. Cut into 2-inch circles with a biscuit cutter or a drinking glass. Place biscuits on prepared cookie sheet. Bake for 20 minutes, or until browned. Serve warm.

MACHO MUSCLE SHAKE

Makes 1 serving

A burst of energy starts your morning with this creamy, high-protein shake. Raw eggs can occasionally cause salmonella — skip the egg or use Egg Beaters if you're concerned.

1 egg
1 oz. vanilla-flavored powdered protein drink mix
1 oz. creamy peanut butter
1 oz. honey
½ ripe banana, cut into chunks
6 oz. orange juice

Combine all ingredients in a blender container. Blend for 1 minute, or until smooth. Pour in a large glass and serve.

PINEAPPLE-BANANA JUPITER

Makes 2–3 servings

A summery drink that can be made year-round to brighten your mood, this is also very healthy.

²⁄₃ cup milk
¹⁄₂ cup cold water
¹⁄₂ can (6 oz.) frozen pineapple juice concentrate
1 tbs. honey
¹⁄₂ tsp. vanilla extract
1 banana, cut into small pieces
6–8 ice cubes
ground allspice

In a blender container, combine milk, water, juice concentrate, honey, vanilla and banana. With the blender running, add ice cubes, 1 at a time, through opening in lid. Blend until smooth. Sprinkle ground allspice on top of each serving. Serve immediately.

PINEANA SHAKE

Makes 1 serving

Try this drink for a nutritious start to your day, or add ice cream for a delicious dessert. It's easy to increase the quantities.

1 ripe banana, sliced (reserve 1 slice for garnish)
3/4 cup cold milk
1/4 cup pineapple juice
ice cream for topping, optional
cinnamon or nutmeg for sprinkling, optional

Place banana into a medium bowl; mash, then beat until smooth and creamy. Add milk and pineapple juice; beat until well mixed. Pour into a glass. If desired, top with a scoop of ice cream or sprinkle with cinnamon or nutmeg. Place a banana slice on edge of glass.

BANANA EGGNOG

This version of the classic holiday drink will delight your guests. Add rum for a grown-up version. Raw eggs can occasionally cause salmonella — use Egg Beaters if you're concerned.

6 eggs, separated
1 cup sugar
8 ripe bananas, mashed
3 qt. milk
1 tbs. vanilla extract
grated fresh ginger, for garnish, optional

In a large bowl, beat egg yolks until blended; gradually beat in sugar. Beat until thick and pale yellow. Blend bananas into yolk mixture. Add milk and extract; mix well. In a separate bowl, beat egg whites until they stand in soft peaks. Fold into banana mixture. Mix well. Cover and refrigerate. Serve in mugs; garnish with grated fresh ginger, if desired.

BANANA SMOOTHIE

Makes 4 servings

This can serve as a morning pick-me-up (without the ice cream) or as an end-of-day relaxer.

4 ripe bananas, mashed
3 cups cold milk
½ cup whipping cream
2 tsp. vanilla extract
1 pint vanilla ice cream, optional
4 slices banana, for garnish

In a large bowl, beat bananas until smooth. Add milk, cream and vanilla; beat until well mixed. Pour into 4 glasses. Float 1 scoop of vanilla ice cream in each glass, if desired, and garnish with a banana slice.

POMEGRANATE BANANA SMOOTHIE

Makes 4 servings

Tangy and creamy, this smoothie is the color of sunset.

2 cups nonfat plain yogurt, chilled
2 cups pure pomegranate juice (fresh-squeezed or bottled), chilled
2 large bananas, thickly sliced
1/4 tsp. ground ginger

In a blender container, combine all ingredients and puree. Pour the smoothies into tall, chilled glasses and serve at once.

BANANA PEANUT BUTTER SMOOTHIE

Makes 1–2 servings

This smoothie is just what you need in the morning. The peanut butter gives it a creamy texture and a bit of protein.

1 cup apple juice, chilled
1 tbs. creamy peanut butter
1 ripe large banana, thickly sliced
1 tsp. honey

In a blender container, combine all ingredients and puree. Pour the smoothies into glasses. Serve at once.

BANANA LOVER'S EGGNOG

Makes 2 servings

A lovely drink for the winter holidays. Raw eggs can occasionally cause salmonella — skip the egg or use Egg Beaters if you're concerned.

1 egg
1 tbs. maple syrup
1/4 tsp. rum flavoring
1 banana, diced
1 cup milk

Combine egg, maple syrup, rum flavoring and banana in a blender container and process until smooth. Add milk and process for another few seconds, or until well mixed. Refrigerate, or serve immediately.

CRANANA SLUSH

This adult beverage is delicious, easy to fix, and a huge hit at parties.

1 can (6 oz.) frozen cranberry juice cocktail concentrate
3/4 cup light rum
1 medium banana, cut into chunks
2 tbs. lemon juice
4 cups crushed ice
craisins (dried cranberries), for garnish, optional
banana slices, for garnish, optional

In a blender container, mix cranberry juice concentrate, rum, banana and lemon juice. Cover and blend until smooth. Add half the ice, cover and blend until smooth. Add the remaining ice, cover and blend until slushy. Pour into glasses. Garnish with a few craisins and banana slices, if desired.

PARTY PUNCH

Kids will love this punch. Try apricot nectar if you can't find papaya juice in your grocery store.

5¾ cups pineapple juice
5¾ cups papaya juice
4 cups mashed ripe bananas
4 cups orange juice
2 qt. orange sherbet
1 pint vanilla ice cream
1 pkg. (10 oz.) frozen strawberries, thawed
2 qt. ginger ale, chilled
1 cup cubed pineapple, for garnish, optional

Combine pineapple juice, papaya juice and orange juice in a large punch bowl. Beat bananas, sherbet and ice cream in with a whisk, leaving small pieces. Add strawberries. Gently stir in ginger ale. Garnish with pineapple cubes, if desired.

HONEY FRUIT PUNCH

Makes about 32 servings

Fragrant honey makes this fruit punch special, and the slushy consistency is fun for all.

4 cups honey
6 cups water
5 bananas, sliced
1 cup orange juice
2 tbs. frozen lemonade
  concentrate

1 large can (28 oz.) unsweetened
  pineapple juice
2 pkg. (10 oz. each) frozen
  strawberries, thawed
few drops red food coloring
2 liters lemon-lime soda

In a large saucepan over medium heat, boil honey and water for 6 minutes; set aside to cool. In a blender container, place bananas, orange juice, lemonade concentrate and pineapple juice; blend until smooth. Pour into a large bowl and stir in honey water. In a small bowl, blend strawberries and food coloring; stir into punch. Freeze mixture for 1 to 3 days before serving. Take out 2 hours before serving to soften. Scoop into punch bowl and add soda just before serving.

BANANA, CHICKEN & COCONUT SOUP

Makes 4 servings

For a tropical treat, try this easily prepared soup. Fish sauce, available in Asian markets, adds a depth of flavor to the soup.

2 cups chicken broth
juice and grated zest of 1 lime
3 tbs. Asian fish sauce
1 tsp. ground ginger
1/2 tsp. chili powder
1 1/4 cups canned coconut milk
6 oz. boneless, skinless chicken breasts, cut into thin strips
2 ripe bananas, coarsely chopped
1/2 cup cooked short-grain rice

Put chicken broth into a saucepan over medium-low heat; add lime juice and zest, fish sauce, ginger and chili powder and simmer for 5 minutes. Add coconut milk and chicken and simmer 5 to 6 minutes, until chicken is just cooked through. Add bananas and rice. Serve hot.

FRUIT SOUP

Makes 10 servings

For breakfast or any other meal, served hot or chilled, this healthy soup is a delicious surprise.

1 cup dried papaya, cut into bite-sized chunks
1 cup dried pineapple, cut into bite-sized chunks
1 cup dried small apricot halves, cut into bite-sized chunks
¼ cup lemon juice
3¼ cups water, divided
1 cup orange juice
1 cup craisins (dried cranberries)
1 tsp. ground ginger
1 tsp. allspice
1 tbs. honey
1 firm banana, cut into small chunks
2 tbs. cornstarch

In a large saucepan combine papaya, pineapple, apricots, lemon juice and 3 cups of the water. Set aside to soak for at least 3 hours.

Add orange juice, craisins, ginger, allspice and honey to the fruit and soaking liquid in the saucepan. Bring mixture to a boil over medium-high heat. Reduce heat to low and simmer, covered, until fruits are tender but still whole. Add banana. In a small bowl, dissolve cornstarch in remaining 1/4 cup cold water. Add to saucepan and cook until soup is thickened, stirring constantly. Serve hot or cover and refrigerate to serve cold.

COLD PAPAYA BANANA SOUP

Makes about 8 servings

What a refreshing lunch on a hot summer day.

2 cups diced dried papaya
2½ cups boiling water
8 very ripe bananas, mashed
2½ qt. milk
1 tbs. sugar

¼ tsp. ground cardamom
grated zest of 2 oranges
2 tsp. cornstarch
2 tsp. cold water

Place dried papaya in a medium bowl and cover with boiling water. Set aside. Combine bananas, milk and sugar in a large saucepan over medium-high heat. Stir in cardamom and orange zest and bring to a boil. Reduce heat to low and simmer 2 minutes. Mix cornstarch with cold water and stir into the soup. Cook, stirring, until thickened. Drain water from papaya and add papaya to soup. Mix well. Remove from heat and set aside to cool to room temperature. Pour into a large bowl; cover and refrigerate for at least 2 hours. Serve cold.

FRUIT SALAD WITH CURAÇAO

Makes 8–10 servings

This fresh fruit salad makes a sophisticated starter (just reduce the amount of sugar) or an elegant, light dessert.

4 peaches, pitted
4 apricots, pitted
1 lb. cherries, pitted
1 pint strawberries, hulled
1 lb. green grapes
4 bananas, sliced
1 small honeydew melon, peeled and cut into chunks
1 cup sugar or honey
1 cup curaçao (orange-flavored) liqueur

Slice peaches and apricots; halve cherries, strawberries and grapes. Combine peaches, apricots, cherries, strawberries, grapes, bananas, and melon in a large glass bowl. Gently stir in sugar and liqueur. Refrigerate before serving.

FRUIT SALAD WITH SHRIMP

Makes 6 servings

This is great to serve for dinner at home or to take to a potluck.

1½ lb. cooked tiny shrimp
2 tbs. lemon juice
2 tbs. lime juice
½ cup shredded coconut
2 firm bananas, sliced
1 can (15¼ oz.) pineapple chunks in juice, drained
½ cup shredded carrots
1 red bell pepper, seeded, chopped
1 green bell pepper, seeded, chopped
Dill Sour Cream Dressing, (recipe follows)

Combine shrimp in a small bowl with lemon juice and lime juice. Toss mixture, cover and refrigerate for up to 1 hour. In a large bowl combine coconut, bananas, pineapple, carrots, red pepper and green pepper. Toss mixture with Dill Sour Cream Dressing. Add shrimp and toss again. Cover bowl and refrigerate for about 1 hour before serving.

DILL SOUR CREAM DRESSING
Makes 1/2 cup

1½ tsp. lemon juice
⅛ tsp. dry mustard
½ cup sour cream

1 pinch cayenne pepper
1 tbs. mayonnaise
2 sprigs fresh dill, chopped

Place all ingredients in a blender container and blend until smooth. Or, using an electric mixer, beat all ingredients in a bowl until smooth. Refrigerate dressing 2 hours before using, to allow flavors to develop.

SWEET POTATO FRUIT SALAD

Makes 6 servings

The dressing enhances this hearty salad's fruitiness.

5 sweet potatoes, baked, peeled
  and diced
4 bananas, sliced
3 golden apples, cored, diced

1 cup craisins (dried cranberries)
2 cups shredded fresh spinach
Pineapple Salad Dressing (recipe
  follows)

Combine sweet potatoes, bananas, apples, craisins and spinach in a large bowl. Toss gently with Pineapple Salad Dressing just before serving.

PINEAPPLE SALAD DRESSING

Makes 2 cups

1/2 cup mayonnaise
2 tbs. lemon juice

1/2 cup flaked coconut
1 cup pineapple-flavored yogurt

Combine mayonnaise and lemon juice. Add coconut and fold in yogurt. Refrigerate before serving.

CHINESE FRUITY CHICKEN SALAD

Makes 6 servings

I made this salad for couple of parties and it was a big hit: everyone requested the recipe.

2 cups cooked, shredded chicken
1/2 head iceberg lettuce, shredded
1/2 red bell pepper, sliced
1 large ripe but firm avocado, peeled, sliced
2 kiwi fruit peeled, cut into chunks
1/2 cup chopped apple
1/2 cup diced dried papaya

1 large ripe banana, sliced into 1/4-inch slices
1/2 tsp. grated fresh ginger
1/4 cup chopped green onions
1 1/2 cup fried chow mein noodles
2 tbs. toasted sesame seeds
Chinese Salad Dressing (recipe follows)

Combine chicken, lettuce, pepper, avocado, kiwi, apple, papaya, banana, ginger, green onions, noodles and sesame seeds in a large bowl. Toss with Chinese Salad Dressing just before serving.

CHINESE SALAD DRESSING

¹/₄ cup rice vinegar
¹/₄ cup vegetable oil
2 tbs. soy sauce
1 tbs. lime juice
2 tbs. honey
¹/₄ tsp. ground black pepper

Whisk together vinegar, oil, soy sauce, lime juice, honey and pepper in a small bowl.

BANANA TORTILLA ROLL

Makes 8 servings

Versatile tortilla rollups are great for breakfast, lunch, or a snack.

1 banana
$1/2$ tsp. allspice
$1/2$ cup applesauce
8 flour tortillas, 8-inch
$1/2$ cup shredded carrots
$1/2$ cup craisins (dried cranberries)
$1/2$ cup honeydew, cut into small cubes
1 cup shredded zucchini

Slice banana in quarters lengthwise. Cut the four pieces in half crosswise; set aside. In a small bowl, combine allspice and applesauce. Set aside. Place 1 banana piece on a tortilla. Sprinkle about $1/8$ each of the carrots, craisins, honeydew and zucchini. Top with 1 tbs. applesauce. Roll up the tortilla. Repeat with remaining tortillas and fillings. Serve immediately.

TURKEY BANANA ROLLUP

Makes 8 servings

Try cutting these tortilla rolls in 1-inch slices as an attractive appetizer for your next gathering.

1 tbs. honey
1/2 cup salad dressing
1/2 tsp. allspice
1 tsp. lemon juice
8 flour tortillas, 8-inch
1 cup shredded fresh spinach

1/2 cup alfalfa sprouts
1 banana, chopped
1/2 cup craisins (dried cranberries)
8 slices cooked turkey

In a small bowl, combine honey, dressing, allspice and lemon juice. Spread about 1 tbs. dressing mixture on a tortilla; sprinkle with about 1/8 each of the spinach, alfalfa sprouts, banana and craisins. Top with a slice of turkey. Roll up tortilla. Repeat with remaining tortillas and fillings. Serve immediately.

LUNCH AND DINNER

CHICKEN AND BANANA CASSEROLE

Makes 6 servings

Serve this zesty springtime casserole over rice.

¼ cup chopped onions
3 tbs. butter
2 tbs. flour
½ tsp. ground mace
⅛ tsp. ground nutmeg
⅛ tsp. garlic powder
1 cup hot prepared chicken gravy

1 cup hot milk
4 cups thickly sliced firm
 bananas
3 cups diced cooked chicken
⅓ cup craisins (dried cranberries)

Heat oven to 375°. Butter a 2-quart casserole dish; set aside. Melt butter in a skillet over medium heat; add onions and sauté for 3 minutes. Blend in flour, mace, nutmeg and garlic powder. Gradually stir in chicken gravy and milk. Cook, stirring constantly, until mixture thickens. Add bananas and chicken. Pour into prepared casserole dish and sprinkle craisins over the top. Bake for 35 minutes and serve at once.

SWEET POTATO BANANA CASSEROLE

Makes 6 servings

This casserole is almost sweet enough to be a dessert. Serve it in place of the usual sweet potato-marshmallow dish.

5 medium sweet potatoes,
  cooked and peeled
ground black pepper, to taste
grated nutmeg, to taste
1/4 tsp. ground cardamom

1/4 cup hot milk
2 firm ripe bananas, mashed
2 egg yolks
2 egg whites, beaten until stiff

Heat oven to 375°. Butter a 2-quart casserole dish; set aside. In a large bowl, mash sweet potatoes, and season to taste with pepper and nutmeg. With an electric mixer, beat in cardamom and hot milk. Add bananas to potatoes. Add egg yolks and beat until mixture is light. Gently fold in egg whites. Pour potato mixture into prepared casserole dish. Bake for 20 minutes or until lightly browned.

JAMAICAN YAM CASSEROLE

Makes 2 servings

Try this casserole for a taste of the islands at your next dinner. The recipe doubles easily.

1 can (1 lb.) yams or sweet potatoes, drained
1/2 banana, thickly sliced
1/4 cup orange juice
1/2 tsp. salt
1/8 tsp. pepper
2 tbs. pecans, coarsely chopped
2 tbs. flaked coconut, toasted

Heat oven to 350°. Butter a 1-quart casserole dish; arrange yams and bananas in the bottom. Pour orange juice over all. Sprinkle with salt and pepper. Top with pecans and coconut. Bake for 30 minutes, covered.

BANANA CITRUS SEAFOOD STEW

Makes 4 servings

8 oz. white skinless fish fillets
4 oz. medium shrimp, peeled and deveined
1 can (14$\frac{1}{2}$ oz.) no-salt-added diced tomatoes, undrained
1 can (14$\frac{1}{2}$ oz.) fat-free, less sodium chicken broth
$\frac{1}{2}$ cup long-grain rice
2 tsp. chili powder
2 cloves garlic, minced
$\frac{1}{2}$ cup tomato paste
$\frac{1}{4}$ cup mashed ripe banana
$\frac{3}{4}$ cup frozen orange-pineapple juice concentrate
1 cup frozen packaged mixed bell peppers with onion
2 firm bananas, cut into $\frac{1}{2}$-inch slices and gently tossed in a little
   lemon juice

Rinse fish and shrimp. Cut fish into 1-inch pieces; set aside in refrigerator. In a large saucepan over high heat, combine tomatoes with their liquid and chicken broth. Bring to a boil. Add rice, chili powder, and garlic. Return to a boil. Reduce heat to low, cover and simmer for about 20 minutes, or until rice is tender, stirring occasionally.

Stir in tomato paste, mashed banana, juice concentrate and frozen pepper mixture. Add fish and shrimp. Raise heat to high until stew boils. Immediately reduce heat to low, cover and simmer gently for 3 to 5 minutes, or until fish flakes easily and shrimp turn pink. Stir in banana slices and remove from heat. Serve hot.

TROPICAL FRUIT STIR-FRY

Makes 6–8 servings

Curry is the perfect sweet-hot balance with the pork and fruit in this recipe.

1 can (20 oz.) pineapple chunks
   in juice
2 tbs. vegetable oil
1 can (4 oz.) chopped green
   chiles, drained
1 small mild red onion, chopped
1 small green bell pepper, cut
   into 1/4-inch strips
1/4 lb. mushrooms, thinly sliced
2 cups chopped cooked pork
2 tbs. curry powder

1 tsp. minced lemon zest
2 firm ripe bananas, cut into
   1-inch slices
1 tsp. anchovy paste
1 cup vegetable broth
2 tbs. cornstarch
1 pkg. (2 1/2 oz.) slivered almonds
1 can (4 oz.) pimientos, drained,
   cut into thin strips
4 cups hot cooked rice

Drain pineapple, reserving ¼ cup juice in a small bowl; set aside. Heat oil in a wok over medium heat. Add chiles, onion, green pepper and mushrooms. Cook, stirring, until onion is soft, 2 to 3 minutes. Add pork and stir-fry until hot, 1 to 2 minutes. Stir in curry powder and lemon zest. Add drained pineapple, bananas, anchovy paste and broth. Stirring gently, raise heat to high and bring to a boil. Combine cornstarch and reserved pineapple juice. Stir into pork mixture and cook until sauce thickens. Stir in almonds and pimientos. Serve over rice.

STIR-FRY SHRIMP AND BANANAS

Makes 6 servings

This stir-fry will have guests asking for more.Check Asian markets for preserved ginger; if you can't find it, use crystallized ginger instead.

2 tbs. butter
2 onions, chopped
1 clove garlic, minced
2 tsp. curry powder
1 tbs. preserved ginger, minced
1 tbs. cider vinegar
$\frac{1}{2}$ tsp. allspice

$1\frac{1}{2}$ lb. shrimp, peeled, deveined
1 cup apple juice
1 tbs. cornstarch mixed with a
   little cold water
4 ripe bananas, cut into $\frac{1}{2}$-inch
   slices, and tossed in a little
   lemon juice

In a wok or large saucepan, melt butter over medium heat. Add onions and garlic and stir-fry until translucent. Stir in curry, ginger, vinegar and allspice. Add shrimp and cook, stirring constantly, until shrimp are just barely pink. Add apple juice and cornstarch and cook mixture, stirring constantly, until thickened and smooth. Add bananas, stirring gently, and cook until just heated through.

PINEAPPLE BANANA CHICKEN STIR-FRY

Makes 6 servings

The sweet-sour sauce adds a punch of flavor without heat.

¼ cup light soy sauce
2 tbs. sugar
1 tbs. cider vinegar
1 tbs. ketchup
½ tsp. ground ginger
2 garlic cloves, minced
1 lb. boneless, skinless chicken
   breast, cut into strips

2 tbs. vegetable oil
1 pkg. (16 oz.) frozen stir-fry
   vegetables
2 cups minced fresh pineapple
   (or canned in juice, drained)
1 ripe banana, chopped
4 cups hot cooked rice

In a small bowl combine soy sauce, sugar, vinegar, ketchup, ginger and garlic; set aside. In a large skillet or wok over medium-high heat, stir-fry chicken in oil for 5 to 6 minutes till juices run clear. Add vegetables and stir-fry 3 to 4 minutes till crisp-tender. Stir in pineapple, banana and soy sauce mixture. Cook just until heated through. Serve over hot rice.

RICE AND BANANAS

Makes 4 servings

A light and satisfying side dish that is an excellent accompaniment to chicken or fish.

1 cup medium-grain rice
1 chicken bouillon cube
2 cups water
2 firm bananas, quartered lengthwise and chopped

In a saucepan over high heat, combine rice, bouillon cube and water. Bring to a boil, stirring to dissolve bouillon cube. Reduce heat to low and simmer, covered, for 15 minutes, or until rice is tender and liquid is absorbed. With two forks, gently toss bananas into hot rice and serve.

FRIED RICE WITH HAM AND BANANAS

Makes 6 servings

Kids will love this great, fruity-tasting, quick dinner.

2 tbs. olive oil
2 cups diced ham, prefer low-sodium
1 cup chopped red bell pepper
3/4 cup thinly sliced green onions
1 cup green peas
1/4 lb. snow peas, trimmed, cut lengthwise into thin strips
4 cups cooked brown rice

2 tbs. chopped fresh cilantro, or 2 tsp. dried
1 can (15 1/4 oz.) pineapple chunks in juice, drained
2 firm ripe bananas, cut into 1-inch slices
1/4 cup low-sodium soy sauce

Heat oil in a large pan over medium-high heat. Add ham, pepper and onions and sauté for about 2 minutes. Add green peas and snow peas and sauté for about 30 seconds. Stir in rice and cook for 2 minutes. Add cilantro and pineapple; cook for 1 minute, stirring gently. Remove from heat. Stir in bananas and soy sauce. Serve hot.

HAWAIIAN RICE

Makes 4 servings

So unique yet so popular, guests will be asking for seconds.

2 tsp. vegetable oil
1 firm banana, cut into cubes
1 small green bell pepper, diced
1 small red bell pepper, diced
1 medium onion, diced
1 can (8 oz.) pineapple chunks in juice
2 tbs. chopped fresh basil, or 2 tsp. dried
1/4 tsp. ground ginger
3 oz. lean cooked ham, cut into cubes
1/2 cup diced water chestnuts
2 cups cooked rice
light soy sauce
ground black pepper

Place wok over medium heat. When hot, add oil, banana, bell peppers and onion; stir-fry for 1 minute. Drain juice from pineapple, reserving pineapple; sprinkle about 2 tbs. juice over hot banana mixture. Reserve remaining juice for another use. Cover and steam 2 minutes until banana gives off some liquid. Increase heat to high; add basil, ginger, ham, pineapple and water chestnuts; stir-fry 30 seconds. Stir in rice, lifting and tossing until ingredients are hot. Season to taste with soy sauce and black pepper.

BANANA TURKEY FRIED RICE

Makes 4 servings

This recipe makes a quick and easy dinner on a busy weeknight.

1 can (15¼ oz.) pineapple chunks in juice
3 tbs. cornstarch, divided
2 tbs. plus ¼ cup soy sauce, divided
2 tsp. minced fresh ginger
1 lb. turkey tenderloins, cut into thin strips
2 tbs. olive oil
½ lb. fresh snow peas, trimmed
1 red bell pepper, chopped
3 cups cooked rice
2 ripe bananas, cut into ½-inch slices, and gently tossed in a little
  lemon juice

Drain pineapple, reserving ½ cup juice. In a small bowl, combine reserved juice with 1 tbs. of the cornstarch and ¼ cup of the soy sauce; mix well and set aside.

In a separate bowl, combine remaining 2 tbs. cornstarch, remaining 2 tbs. soy sauce and ginger and coat turkey tenderloins with mixture; marinate for a few minutes. Heat oil in a large skillet over medium-high heat. Add turkey; cook, stirring frequently, 4 to 6 minutes until turkey is cooked through. Add snow peas and bell pepper and stir-fry 1 to 2 minutes. Add soy sauce mixture and pineapple. Cook, stirring constantly, until sauce boils and thickens slightly. Stir in rice and bananas; cook 2 minutes longer until the rice mixture is hot.

BANANA, WILD RICE, CHICKEN AND APPLE HASH

Makes 2 servings

Substitute smoked turkey or even ham for an equally delicious dish.

1 cup cooked wild rice
1 cup cooked brown rice
1 green onion, thinly sliced
1 small apple, peeled and
   coarsely chopped
2 tbs. flour
1 egg, beaten

1/2 tsp. baking powder
1/8 tsp. ground cardamom
1/4 tsp. ground black pepper
6 oz. smoked chicken, finely
   chopped
1 tbs. olive oil
1 ripe banana, sliced

Combine wild rice, brown rice, onion, apple, flour, egg, baking powder, cardamom, pepper and chicken in a medium bowl. Heat oil in a large nonstick skillet over medium heat. Add hash mixture. Cook until lightly browned, stirring occasionally. Serve with banana slices on top.

BANANA BREAD

Makes 1 loaf

Banana bread is a staple in any household; this one is low-fat and fabulous.

3 ripe bananas
2 eggs, well beaten
2 tbs. melted butter or margarine
2 cups flour
3/4 cup sugar, or 1/2 cup honey
1 tsp. baking soda
1/2 cup coarsely chopped pecans

Heat oven to 350°. Grease and flour a 9 x 5-inch loaf pan. In a large bowl, mash bananas well and mix with eggs and melted butter. Stir in flour, sugar and baking soda. Add pecans. Pour batter into prepared loaf pan. Bake bread for 1 hour. Cool for 10 minutes in the pan, then turn bread out onto a rack and cool completely.

BANANA NUT TEA BREAD

Makes 1 loaf

Although pecans or walnuts are traditional (and delicious) in this bread, also try cashews or hazelnuts.

1¾ cup flour
2 tsp. baking powder
¼ tsp. baking soda
⅓ cup shortening

⅔ cup sugar, or ½ cup honey
2 eggs
1 cup mashed ripe bananas
½ cup nuts, coarsely chopped

Heat oven to 350°. Grease and flour a 9 x 5-inch loaf pan. Sift flour, baking powder and baking soda into a small bowl. In a large bowl, using an electric mixer at medium speed, beat shortening with sugar, then with eggs until very light and fluffy, about 4 minutes. At low speed, beat in flour mixture alternately with bananas and nuts just until smooth; pour batter into prepared pan. Bake for 1 hour, or until toothpick inserted in the center comes out clean. Cool in pan for 10 minutes; remove bread to cool completely on a wire rack.

SPICY GINGER BANANA BREAD

Makes 2 loaves

4 eggs
1½ cups brown sugar, packed
1 cup vegetable oil
1½ tsp. vanilla
3 cups flour
1 tsp. baking powder
½ tsp. baking soda
2 tsp. ground cinnamon

½ tsp. each ground nutmeg,
  ginger and mace
¼ tsp. allspice
2 cups mashed bananas
¼ cup minced crystallized ginger
½ cup craisins (dried cranberries)
½ cup chopped pecans

Heat oven to 350°. Grease and flour two 9 x 5-inch loaf pans. Beat eggs in a large bowl. Beat in brown sugar, then beat in oil and vanilla. Sift flour, baking powder, baking soda, cinnamon, nutmeg, ground ginger, mace and allspice in a separate bowl. Add dry mixture to egg mixture and stir lightly. Add banana, crystallized ginger, craisins and pecans and stir well. Pour into prepared pans. Bake for 55 minutes, or until toothpick inserted in center comes out clean.

RUM BANANA RAISIN CAKE

Makes 12 servings

This cake is easy and delicious, and will disappear very quickly.

1 cup mashed ripe bananas
1/4 cup milk
1 1/2 cups sugar
1/2 cup (1 stick) butter, softened
3 eggs
2 1/2 cups flour
1 tsp. baking powder
1/2 tsp. baking soda
1 tsp. allspice
3/4 cup dark rum
1 cup raisins
1 cup coarsely chopped walnuts
confectioner's sugar, for dusting

Heat oven to 350°. Grease and flour a 10-inch tube or bundt pan. In a small bowl, combine bananas with milk. Mix well. In a large bowl, cream sugar and butter until light and fluffy. Beat in eggs one at a time until blended. In a separate bowl, combine flour, baking powder, baking soda and allspice. Beat flour mixture into egg mixture until blended. Beat in banana mixture until blended. Beat in rum until well blended. Stir in raisins and nuts. Pour into prepared pan. Bake for 50 minutes, or until a toothpick inserted in center comes out clean. Cool in pan about 10 minutes; remove cake to cool on wire rack. Dust with confectioner's sugar before serving.

TROPICAL FRUIT PIZZA

This delicious, attractive dessert is best eaten on the same day it's prepared.

1 tube refrigerated sugar cookie
    dough
1 pkg. (8 oz.) cream cheese,
    softened
1 tsp. vanilla extract
1/2 tsp. ground allspice
1 cup sugar, divided
1 cup sliced avocados
1 cup sliced bananas

1/2 cup lemon juice, divided
1 cup sliced kiwi
1 cup crushed pineapple, drained
1/2 cup craisins (dried cranberries)
1/2 cup flaked coconut
3/4 cup water
1 cup orange juice
3 tbs. cornstarch

Heat oven to 350°. Prepare crust: slice cookie dough ⅛ inch thick and press slices onto well-greased pizza pan to cover surface completely. Bake for 10 minutes. Set aside to cool.

In a small bowl, combine cream cheese, vanilla, allspice and ½ cup of the sugar. Spread evenly over cooled crust. Dip avocados and bananas in ¼ cup of the lemon juice to keep from browning. Arrange avocados, bananas, kiwi and pineapple on top of cream cheese layer. Sprinkle craisins and coconut over fruit. In a small saucepan, mix together water, remaining ½ cup sugar, orange juice, remaining ¼ cup lemon juice and cornstarch. Bring to a boil, stirring constantly, until thickened. Cool. Pour over fruit. Refrigerate for 2 hours before serving.

BANANA CREAM PIE

Banana Cream Pie *is a great diner classic that you can easily make at home.*

2 cups milk, divided
3 large egg yolks
1/2 tsp. vanilla extract
3/4 cup sugar
2 tbs. flour
2 tbs. cornstarch
1/4 tsp. ground cardamom
1/8 tsp. grated nutmeg
2 tbs. butter
2 tbs. light rum
3 ripe bananas, sliced 1/4-inch thick
1 baked 9-inch piecrust
whipped cream and sliced fresh or dried bananas, optional, for
    garnish

In a medium bowl, mix ¼ cup of the milk, egg yolks and vanilla; set aside. In a saucepan over medium heat, combine sugar, flour, cornstarch, cardamom and nutmeg. Add remaining 1¾ cups milk and bring to a simmer, whisking constantly. Add butter and cook, stirring, over medium heat until thick and smooth, 2 to 3 minutes. Remove from heat and stir about half of the hot mixture gradually into egg yolk mixture. Pour egg mixture back into hot mixture in saucepan and cook over medium heat, stirring constantly, until thickened, about 3 minutes. Strain through a fine sieve set over a bowl. Add rum and mix well. Cover bowl with plastic wrap; refrigerate just until custard reaches room temperature. Arrange bananas in overlapping layers into piecrust; pour filling over bananas. Refrigerate until serving time. Top pie with whipped cream and garnish with banana slices, if desired.

BANANA BAKED RICE PUDDING

Makes 6 servings

This is a very comforting, traditional dish with an added banana flavor — perfect on a cold winter's evening.

1 qt. milk
1/4 cup sugar
1/2 cup white rice
1 tbs. butter or margarine, melted
1/4 tsp. nutmeg

1/4 tsp. lemon juice
1 tsp. vanilla extract
1 firm banana, cut into small chunks

Heat oven to 325°. Grease a 1½-qt. casserole dish. In a large bowl, combine milk, sugar, rice, butter, nutmeg, lemon juice and vanilla. Pour into prepared dish and bake, uncovered, stirring occasionally, for 1 hour. Stir in banana and return pudding to the oven. Bake 1½ hours longer, or until rice is very soft and pudding is thick. Serve warm or cold, with whipped cream or caramel sauce on top.

CHEWY BANANA GRANOLA BARS

Makes 24 bars

Granola bars are great portable snacks. Pack these in your children's lunch boxes for a nutritious treat.

³/₄ cup flour
½ tsp. baking powder
³/₄ cup brown sugar, firmly packed
¼ cup granulated sugar

⅓ cup margarine, melted
2 egg whites
1 ripe banana, mashed
2 cups granola cereal

Heat oven to 350°. Grease a 9-inch square baking pan. In a small bowl, stir together flour and baking powder. In a medium bowl, beat together sugars, margarine, egg whites and banana until well blended. Stir in flour mixture, mixing until well combined. Stir in granola cereal. Spread evenly into prepared pan. Bake for 25 to 30 minutes or until lightly browned. Cool completely before cutting. Cut into small squares. Store in an airtight container at room temperature.

SPICY BANANA BARS

These bars are packed with flavor. Find soy flour in health food stores. If you can't find poppy seed flour, you may grind whole poppy seeds for a similar result.

1 cup whole wheat flour
¼ cup poppy seed flour
1 cup soy flour
1 cup nonfat dry milk
3 tsp. baking powder
1 tsp. allspice
½ cup walnuts, chopped
¼ cup sunflower seeds, unsalted, chopped
1½ cups mashed ripe bananas
2 eggs
½ cup safflower or vegetable oil
½ cup buttermilk
1 cup brown sugar, packed

Heat oven to 350°. Grease and flour a 9 x 13-inch baking pan. Mix flours, dry milk, baking powder, allspice, walnuts and sunflower seeds together in a medium bowl. In a large bowl, combine bananas, eggs, oil, buttermilk and sugar. Beat until well mixed. Add dry ingredients and mix until just moistened. Pour batter into prepared pan. Bake for 35 to 45 minutes, or until cake shrinks slightly from sides of pan. Cool completely before cutting into bars.

BANANA RUM ICE CREAM

Makes 4–6 servings

Easy banana ice cream is just an hour away. Raw eggs can occasionally cause salmonella; if you're concerned, you can use Egg Beaters.

2 eggs
1/2 cup sugar
1/4 cup honey
2 cups mashed ripe bananas
1 tbs. lemon juice
2 cups half-and-half
1 cup whipping cream
3 tbs. rum

In a large bowl, beat eggs until blended. Beat in sugar and honey until mixture is smooth and light. Stir in bananas and lemon juice. Stir in half-and-half, whipping cream and rum. Freeze in ice cream maker according to manufacturer's directions.

BANANA PAPAYA POPSICLES

Children love making these popsicles, and even adults will enjoy them.

1 envelope unflavored gelatin
³/₄ cup pineapple-orange banana juice concentrate (pourable)
1³/₄ cups diced bananas
³/₄ cup diced fresh papaya
16 oz. banana-flavored nonfat yogurt

In a saucepan, sprinkle gelatin over juice concentrate. Let stand 1 minute until gelatin softens. Cook over low heat, stirring, for 2 minutes, or until gelatin dissolves. Combine bananas, papaya, yogurt and gelatin mixture in a food processor workbowl or blender container. Process until smooth. Spoon mixture evenly into 3-ounce popsicle molds or paper cups. If using paper cups, cover openings with aluminum foil, and insert a popsicle stick through the foil into the center of each cup. Freeze until firm. Remove aluminum foil, unmold popsicles and serve.

AVOCADO BANANA POPSICLES

Makes 6–8 popsicles

These have an exciting taste—terrific for a picnic or birthday party.

1 can (6 oz.) frozen orange juice concentrate, thawed
1/4 cup water
1 envelope unflavored gelatin

1 3/4 cups diced bananas
3/4 cup diced avocado
16 oz. banana-flavored nonfat yogurt

In a small saucepan, combine juice concentrate with water; sprinkle gelatin over top. Let stand 1 minute until gelatin softens. Cook over low heat, stirring, for about 2 minutes, or until gelatin dissolves. Combine bananas, avocado, yogurt and gelatin mixture in a food processor workbowl or blender container. Process until smooth. Spoon mixture evenly into 3-ounce popsicle molds or paper cups. If using paper cups, cover opening with aluminum foil and insert a popsicle stick through the foil into the center of each cup. Freeze until firm. Remove aluminum foil, unmold popsicles and serve.

BANANA HONEY SAUCE

Makes about 4 cups

Here's a sauce that can go with savory or sweet dishes. It will spark up the taste of salads, or you can serve it over cakes and ice cream.

2 cups mashed ripe bananas
3 tbs. honey
2 tsp. lemon juice
1 cup whipping cream
1/3 cup chopped nuts

In a small bowl, combine bananas, honey and lemon juice. Mix well. In a separate bowl, whip cream until stiff. Fold in banana mixture until well blended. Add nuts.

APPLE BANANA PAPAYA SALSA

Makes about 6 cups

This is a lovely topping over rice, or grilled chicken, fish or pork.

4 serrano chiles, preferably yellow
  or red, stemmed, seeded
1 large yellow onion, chopped
  (about 2 cups)
1½ cups diced fresh pineapple,
  divided
¼ cup pineapple juice
1½ tsp. turmeric
½ tsp. ground coriander seed
½ tsp. ground mace
1 tbs. ground cumin
½ tsp. cayenne pepper
1 tsp. red chili powder

1½ tsp. ground black pepper
1-inch piece fresh ginger, minced
¼ tsp. cornstarch
¼ cup cider vinegar
2 tsp. honey
2 firm bananas, cut into ½-inch
  cubes
1 ripe papaya, peeled and diced
1 golden apple, diced
1 red apple, diced
6 tbs. lime juice
1 small red onion, finely chopped
1 clove garlic, minced

Sterilize eight 6-oz. canning jars and lids. Place the chiles, yellow onion, 1 cup of the pineapple, pineapple juice, turmeric, coriander, mace, cumin, cayenne, chili powder, pepper and ginger in a blender container and puree until very smooth. In large saucepan over low heat, dissolve cornstarch in the vinegar, add the puree and honey and simmer slowly for 10 minutes. In a large bowl, combine bananas, papaya, remaining ½ cup pineapple and apples with lime juice, red onion and garlic. Stir until well coated with lime juice. Add fruit mixture to puree in saucepan and simmer 5 minutes. Cool slightly and pour into prepared jars. Leave ¼-inch headspace. Wipe rims clean and screw on lids. Invert jars for 5 minutes. Turn jars upright and cool to room temperature. Store in the refrigerator. Refrigerated, the salsa will keep up to 8 weeks.

PEACH BANANA JAM

Makes about 6 cups

This can be served as a tangy-sweet condiment with chicken or fish, or as a dessert topping.

5 firm bananas, thinly sliced
1 lb. peaches, peeled, pitted and
   coarsely chopped
1 cup lime juice

2 tbs. lemon juice
$2\frac{1}{2}$–3 cups sugar, to taste
$\frac{1}{2}$ tsp. vanilla extract
1 cinnamon stick (3 inches long)

Sterilize eight 6-oz. canning jars and lids. Combine all ingredients in a large, heavy saucepan over high heat. Bring to a boil. Reduce heat to medium-low and simmer, stirring often, for 30 minutes, or until thick. Taste and add more sugar, if desired. Remove cinnamon and discard. Spoon hot jam into prepared jars. Leave $\frac{1}{4}$ inch headspace. Wipe rims clean and screw on lids. Invert jars for 5 minutes. Turn jars upright and cool to room temperature. Store in the refrigerator. Once opened, jam will keep in the refrigerator for up to 3 weeks.

GUAVA BANANA JAM

Makes 5 cups

This tastes wonderful on bagels and toast; or use it to make peanut butter and jam sandwiches with an exotic flair.

6 guavas, peeled, seeded and
    mashed
4 firm bananas, peeled and
    mashed

¾ cup pineapple juice
¼ cup lemon juice
3 apples, halved
4 cups sugar

Sterilize five 8-oz. canning jars and lids. In a large saucepan, combine guavas, bananas, pineapple juice, lemon juice and apples. Bring to a boil and then add sugar; stir to dissolve, reduce heat to low and simmer for 30 minutes. Remove apples and discard. Spoon jam into prepared jars. Leave ¼-inch headspace. Wipe rims clean and screw on lids. Invert jars for 5 minutes. Turn jars upright and cool to room temperature. Store jam in the refrigerator. Once opened, jam will keep in refrigerator for up to 3 weeks.

INDEX